PIANO | VOCAL | GUITAR

THE LUMINEERS

CLEOPATRA

2 SLEEP ON THE FLOOR

10 OPHELIA

16 CLEOPATRA

25 GUN SONG

32 ANGELA

39 IN THE LIGHT

45 GALE SONG

52 LONG WAY FROM HOME

55 SICK IN THE HEAD

60 MY EYES

64 PATIENCE

67 WHERE THE SKIES ARE BLUE

71 EVERYONE REQUIRES A PLAN

75 WHITE LIE

ISBN 978-1-4950-6902-4

7777 W. BLUEMOUND RD. P.O. BOX 13819 MILWAUKEE, WI 53213

Visit Hal Leonard Online at
www.halleonard.com

SLEEP ON THE FLOOR

Words and Music by JEREMY FRAITES
and WESLEY SCHULTZ

F
C
take all of your sav - ings out.
'Cause if we don't
Am
G
F
C
leave this town
we might nev - er make it out.
Am
G
I was not born to drown.
Ba - by, come on.
C
F
C
For - get what Fa - ther

F
C
Bren - nan said, we were not born in sin.
Leave a note on your bed, let your moth - er
F
C
Am
G
know you're safe. And by the time she wakes
F
C
we'll have driv - en through the state, we'll have driv - en

Am
G
through the night.
Ba - by, come on.
C
If the
sun don't shine on me to - day, and if the
lay your - self down and dig your grave, or will you
F
Am
G
1
C
sub - ways flood and bridg - es break,
will you
rail a - gainst the dy - ing

2
C
day?
And when we
looked out - side,
could - n't e - ven see the sky.
F
C
How do you pay the rent?
Is it your
par - ents,
or is it hard work, dear,
F
C
Am
G

F C
hold - ing the at - mos - phere? I don't wan - na
Am G C
live like that. If the sun don't shine on
F Am
me to - day, if the sub - ways flood and the
G(add4) Am C F
bridg - es break,... Je - sus Christ can't save

Am
G
C
Am
G/B
C
F
me to - night.
Put on your dress, yes, wear
some - thing nice.
de - cide on me, yeah, de - cide
on us.
Oh,
Il - li - nois,
Il - li - nois.

Pack your - self a tooth - brush, dear,
pack your - self a
F
C
fa - v'rite blouse.
Take a with - draw - al slip,
take all of your sav - ings out,
'cause if we don't
Am
G
leave this town,
we might nev - er make it out.
3
rit.

OPHELIA

Words and Music by JEREMY FRAITES
and WESLEY SCHULTZ

B♭
F
Dm
B♭
noth - ing back.
F
Dm
B♭
F
Dm
B♭
F
I, I've got a new girl - friend. She
Dm
B♭
F
feels like he's on top. And I

C
B♭
F
don't feel no re-morse.
And you
Dm
B♭
F
can't see past my blind - ness.
Dm
B♭
F
C
B♭
Oh, O - phe - li - a,
you've been on my mind, girl, since the flood.
F
Dm
B♭
F
C
B♭
To Coda
Oh, O - phe - li - a,
heav-en help the fool who falls in love.

F
Dm
B♭
F
Dm
B♭
F
Dm
B♭
I, I got a lit - tle
F
Dm
pay - check. You got big plans,
B♭
F
and you got - ta move. And I

C
B♭
F
don't feel noth - ing at all.
And you
Dm
B♭
F
can't feel noth - ing small.
"Hon - ey, I
B♭
F
C
F
B♭/F
F
love you," that's all she wrote.
Dm
B♭
F
C
B♭
Oh, O - phe - li - a,
you've been on my mind, girl, like a drug.

F
Dm
B♭
F
Oh, O - phe - li - a,
heav - en help the
C
B♭
F
D.S. al Coda
fool who falls in love.
CODA
F
Dm
B♭
F
C
B♭
F
Oh, O - phe - li - a,
you've been on my mind, girl, like a drug.
Dm
B♭
F
C
B♭
F
Oh, O - phe - li - a,
heav - en help the fool who falls in love.

CLEOPATRA

Words and Music by JEREMY FRAITES,
WESLEY SCHULTZ and SIMONE FELICE

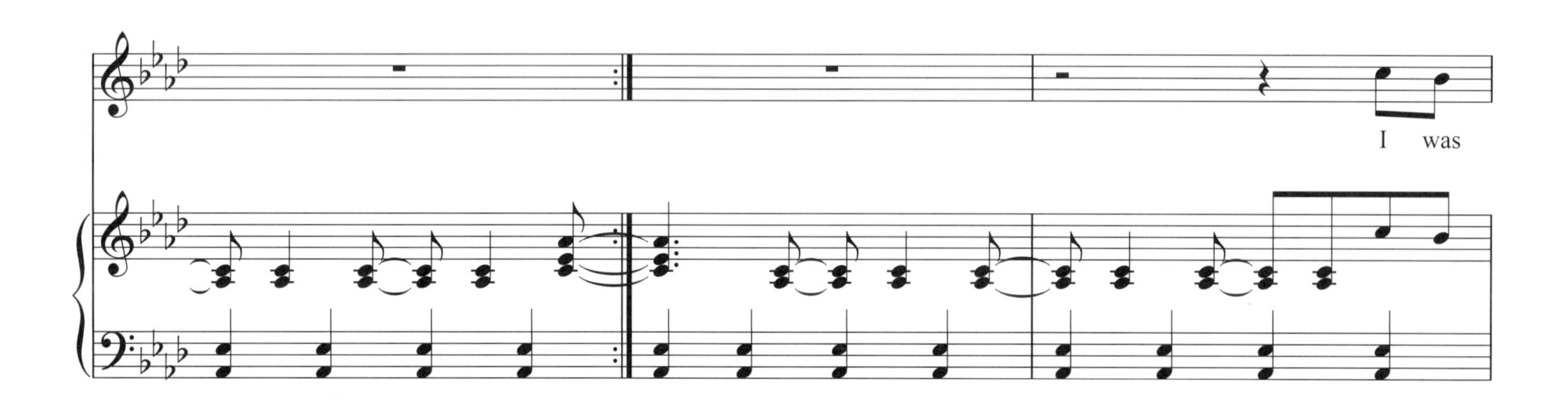

E♭
3fr
E♭sus2
6fr
A♭
4fr
hand. But I was sad you asked __ it, as I laid in a black __ dress. With my
fa - ther in a cas - ket, I had no plans, __
E♭sus2
6fr
yeah. ____
A♭
4fr

And I left the foot -
Db
Ab
4fr
- prints, the mud stained on the car - pet. And it
Ebsus2
6fr
hard - ened like my heart did when you left town.
Ab
4fr
But I must ad - mit it, that I would

D♭
A♭
4fr
mar - ry you __ in an in - stant. Damn your wife, __ I'd be your mis -
E♭sus2
6fr
- tress just to have you a - round. But I was
A♭
E♭
3fr
D♭
late for this, __ late for that. __ Late for the love __ of my __
__ life. __ And when I die a - lone, __ when I die a - lone, __

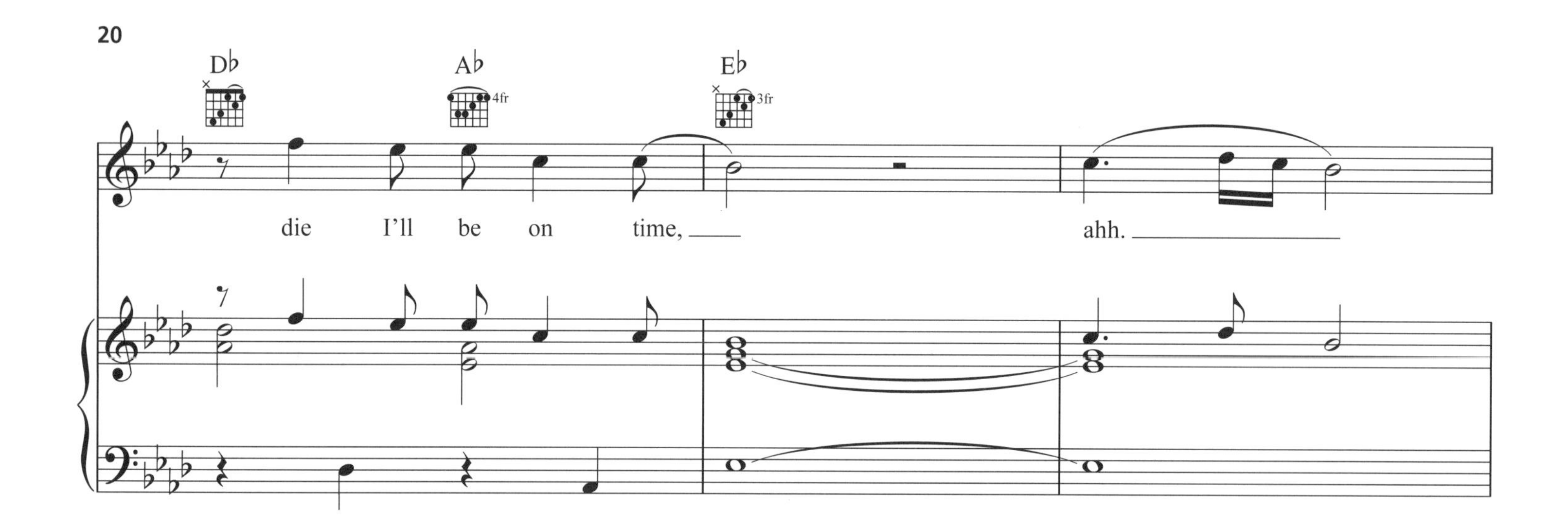
D♭
A♭
4fr
E♭
3fr
die I'll be on time,
ahh.

A♭
4fr

And while the church dis - cour - aged an - y lust

D♭
that burned with - in me. Yes, my flesh, it was not cur -

E♭
3fr
E♭sus2
6fr
ren - cy but I held true.
So I
A♭
4fr
D♭
drive a tax - i and the traf - fic dis - tracts
A♭
4fr
D♭
A♭
4fr
me from the strang - ers in my back seat. They re - mind me of
E♭sus2
6fr
you.
But I was

A♭
E♭
D♭
A♭
D♭
A♭
E♭
late for this, late for that. Late for the love of my life. And when I
A♭
E♭
D♭
A♭
D♭
A♭
To Coda
die a - lone, when I die a - lone, when I die, I'll be on time.
E♭sus2
Fm
The on - ly gifts from my Lord
A♭
D♭
E♭
Fm
were birth and a di - vorce.

A♭
Fm
But I've read this script and the cos - tume fits,
D♭
E♭
A♭
so I'll play my part.
I was Cle - o - pat -
D♭
A♭
- ra, I was tall - er than the raft - ers. But that's

E♭sus2
6fr
all in the past now, gone with the wind.
And now a
A♭
4fr
D♭
A♭
4fr
nurse in white shoes leads me back to my guest - room.
It's a bed
D♭
E♭
3fr
and a bath - room and a place for the end.
freely
D.S. al Coda
I won't be
a tempo
CODA
E♭
3fr
A♭
4fr
ahh.
rit.

GUN SONG

Words and Music by JEREMY FRAITES
and WESLEY SCHULTZ

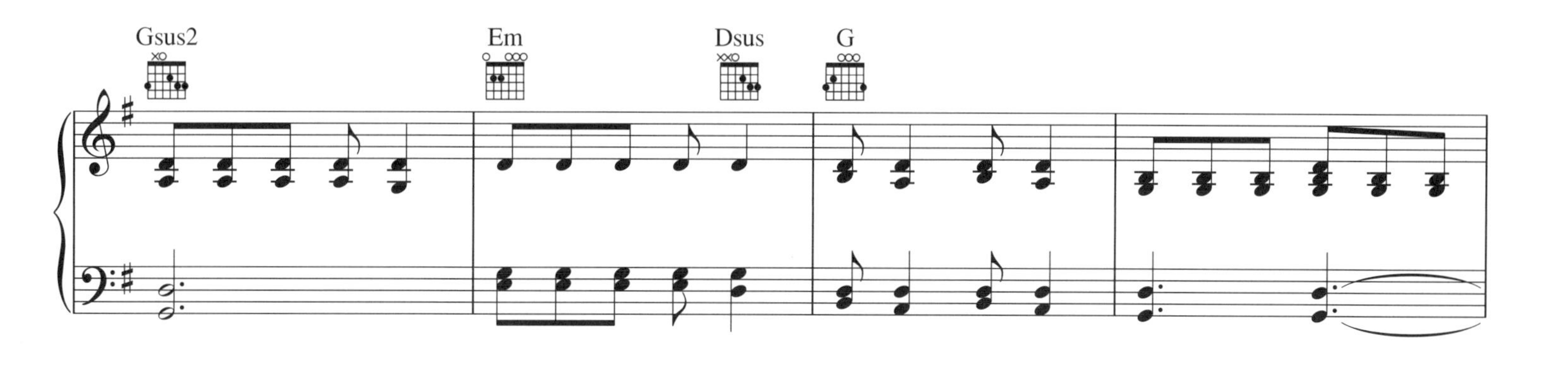

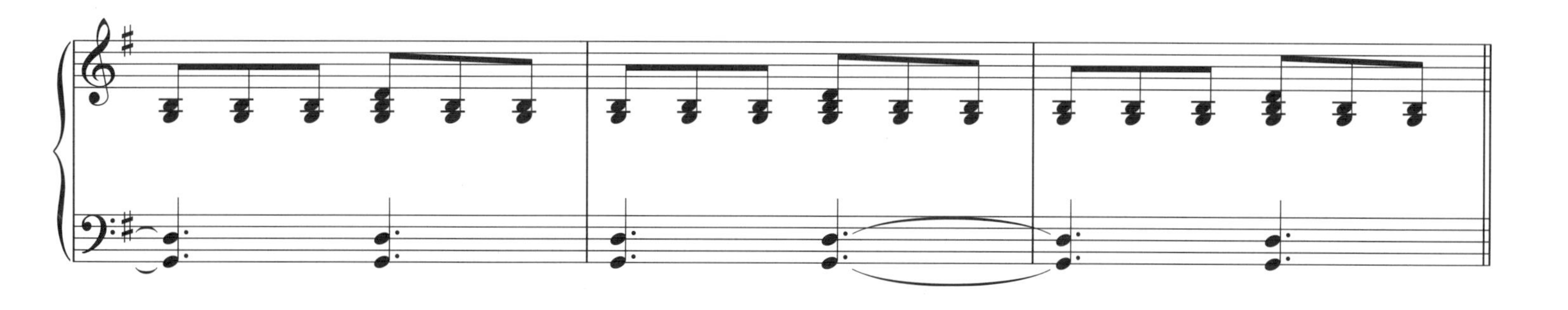

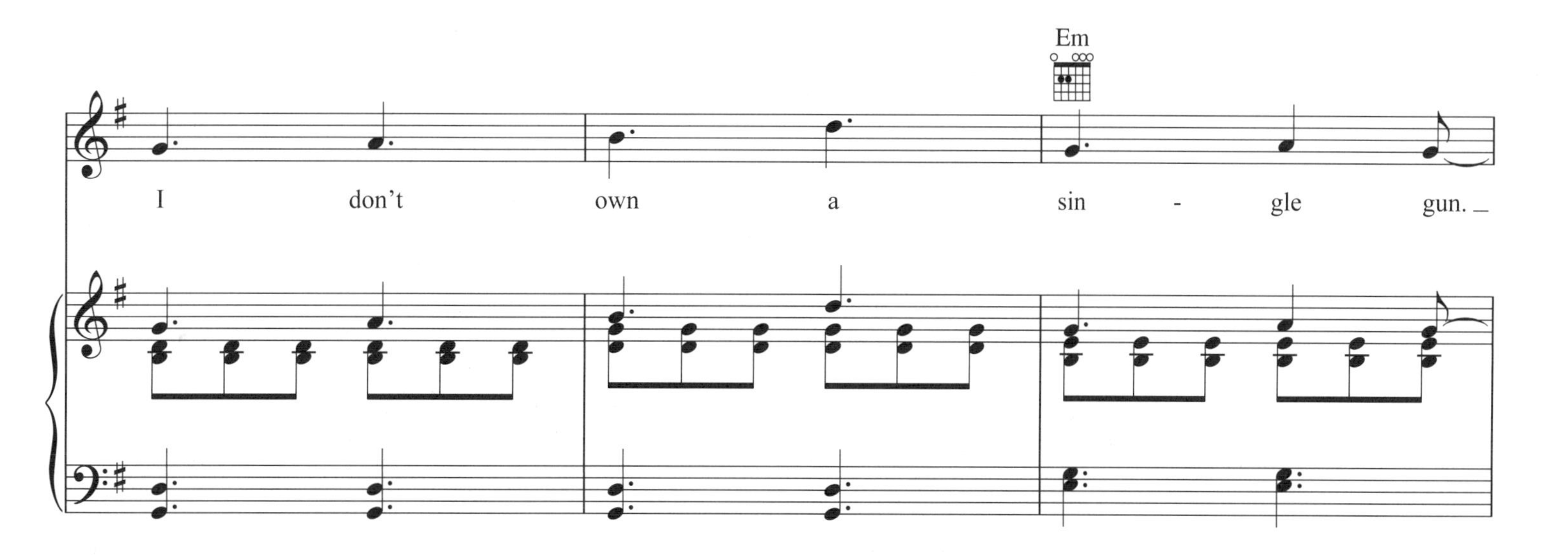

G
But if I did, you'd
Em
G
be the one to hold it, aim it,
Em
D/F♯
G
make all of the bad men run. But
D/F♯
Em
D
C
D
I don't own a sin - gle gun.

G
Gsus2
G6
G
G5
3fr
I don't have a
C
G
sweet - heart yet.
But if I
C
G
did, I'd break my neck

C
D
to please her, make her want to stay, in my arms she'd rest.
G
D/F♯
Em
D
But I don't have a
C
D
G
Gsus2
sweet - heart yet.
I can't be - lieve what
La la la la la
G6
G
I found in dad - dy's sock drawer, sock drawer to - day.
la la la la la la la la la la.

Gsus2
G6
1
G
It was a pis - tol, a Smith and Wes - son, ho - ly, ho - ly shit.
La la la la la la la la la la
2
G
Gsus(add2)
G
G6/9
G
la la la la.
La la la la la la la la la la
1
2
G(add2)
G
la la la la la la. la.
La la la la la
Am/G
G
1
2
la la la la la la la la la la la. la. One!

Two! One, two three!
C
Things I knew when I was young,
G
some were true and some
C
G
were wrong.
And one day, I pray,

C
D
G
D/F♯
I'll be more than my fa - ther's son.
But I don't
Em
D
C
D
G
own a sin - gle gun.
Gsus2
G6
G
La la la la la la la la la la la la la la.
Gsus2
G6
G
La la la la la la la la la la.

ANGELA

Words and Music by JEREMY FRAITES,
WESLEY SCHULTZ and SIMONE FELICE

C
Gm
F/C
ex - its pass, all the tar and glass 'til the road and sky a - lign.
held your course to some dis - tant war in the cor - ners of your mind.
C
Gm
The stran - gers in this town, they
From the sec - ond time a - round, the
F/C
Dm
C
raise you up just to cut you down. Oh, An - ge - la, it's a
on - ly love I ev - er found. Oh, An - ge - la, it's a
Gm
F/C
1
long time com - ing. And your
long time com - ing.

2
C
F
Home at last.
Am
C
Were you safe and warm in your
Gm
3fr
F
coat of arms with your fin - gers in a fist?
Did you
C
Gm
3fr
hear the notes, all those stat - ic codes in the

F
C
ra - di - o a - byss?
The stran - gers in this town,
Gm
3fr
F
Dm
they raised you up just to cut you down. Oh, An -
C
Gm
3fr
F
- ge - la, it's a long time com - ing.
Dm
C
Gm
3fr
Oh, An - ge - la, spent your whole life run - ning a - way.

F
C
Home at last.
F
Am
Home at last.
C
F
Am
To Coda
C
Gm
3fr
Va - can - cy,
ho - tel room,
lost in me,

F/C
C
lost in you. An - ge - la, I'm on my knees,
Gm
3fr
F
D.S. al Coda
I be - long, I be - lieve. Home at last.
CODA
C
F
Home at last.
Am
C
Home at last.

F
Am
Home at last.
C
Gm
3fr
F
Mmm,
mmm.
Dm
C
Gm
3fr
Mmm,
mmm.
Mmm,
F
Dm
C
mmm.

IN THE LIGHT

Words and Music by JEREMY FRAITES
and WESLEY SCHULTZ

Dmaj7
B9
A
Mmm.
A
Mem - 'ries old, but I
I don't know why I
just can't let it go.
just can't let it go.
The
To Coda
i - dea's gone, but I just can't let it go.
Mem - 'ry's old, but I just can't let it go.

A
D/A
A
D/A
A
D/A
A
D/A
A
D/A
A
D/A
A
F♯m
A
D/A
A
D/A
A
D/A
A
Time,
give me my
Fate
dealt you a
C♯
C♯sus
C♯
C♯sus
C♯
C♯sus
C♯
D
4fr
yes - ter - days.
Save it for
all you had
in your eyes,
trick - y hand.
Now you're just
left a - lone
in your mind
1
B9
A
D/A
A
D/A
A
D/A
A
I have gone a - way.

2
B9
A
and I have gone a - way.
Mmm.
D.S. al Coda
CODA
A
D/A
A
D/A
A
D/A
A
D/A
A
D/A
A
1
D/A
A
2
D/A
A
In the light,

F♯m
E6
D
A
F♯m
E6
right here in the light.
D
A
F♯m
E6
D
Right here in the, hold me and don't you ev - er let this die.
B
D
A
F♯m
E6
Right here in the light.
D
A
F♯m
E6
D
In the day - time.
Right here in the,

A
F♯m
E6
D
hold me and don't you ev - er let this die.
D7/C
In the light.
In the day - time,
E
right here in the...
B

GALE SONG

from THE HUNGER GAMES: CATCHING FIRE

Words and Music by JEREMY FRAITES,
WESLEY SCHULTZ and NEYLA PEKAREK

F
C
F/C
C
Am
home in spring,
I can wait 'til
C
F/C
C
F/A
G6
then.
I heard you're on the
F
C
F/C
C
big train.
And
F
C
all of this shall pass.

F
This lone - li - ness won't last
C
G
Am
for long.
I was - n't there
G
F
C
to take his place.
Am
G
F
C
I was ten thous - and miles a - way.

F C F/C
So when you hear my voice,
C Am C F/C C
when you say my name, may it
F/A G6 C F/C C
nev - er be in pain. And I don't
F C F/C C Am C F/C
want to go but it's time to leave.

C F/A G6 C F/C
You'll be on my mind, in my des - ti - ny.
C F C
And I won't fight in vain.
F
I love you just the same.
C G Am G F
Ooh. I could-n't know what's in your mind.

C
Am
G
F
But I saw the pic-tures, you're look-ing fine.
C
And there was a time when I stood in line for love,
G
F
for love, for love. But I let you go, oh,
C
I let you go. And he

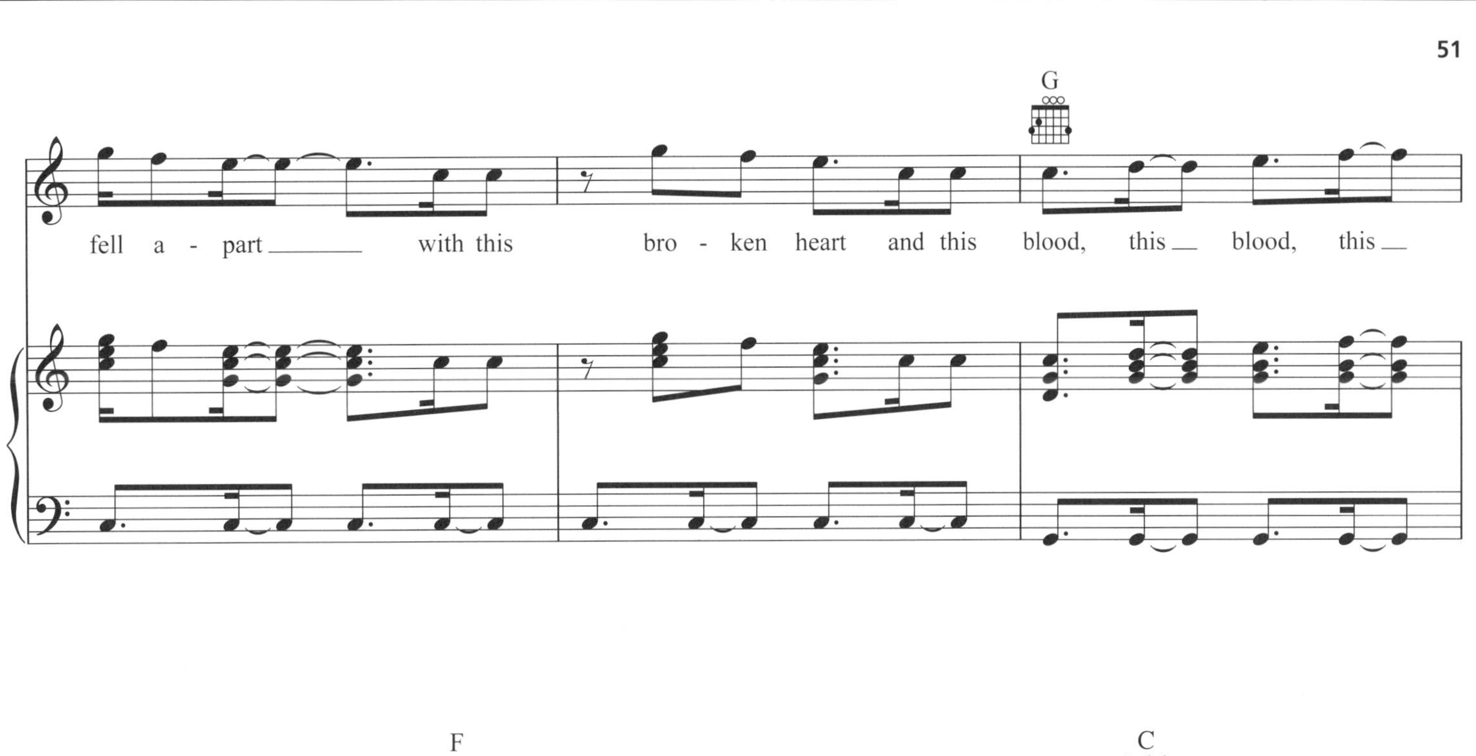
G
fell a - part with this bro - ken heart and this blood, this blood, this

F
C
blood. Oh, it drains from my skin and dust.

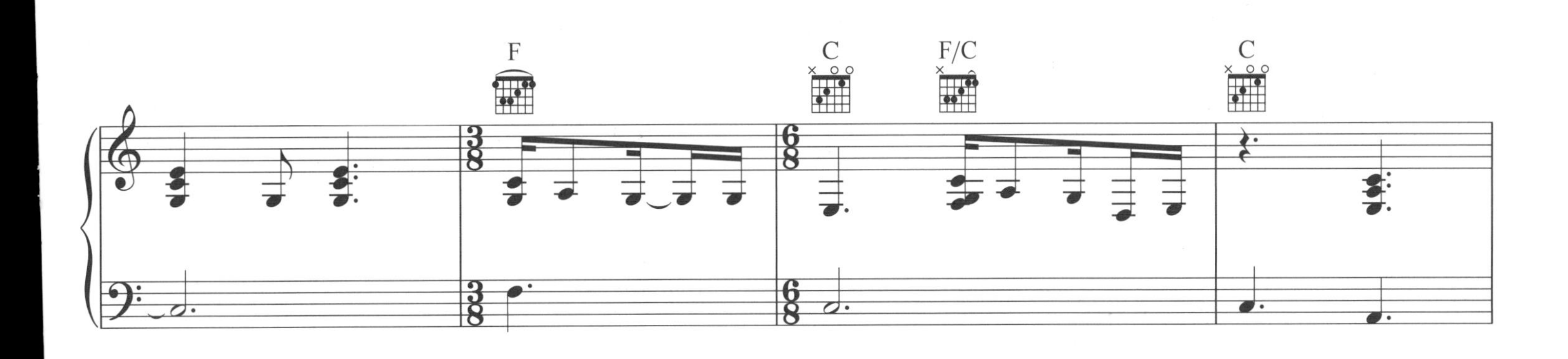
F
C
F/C
C

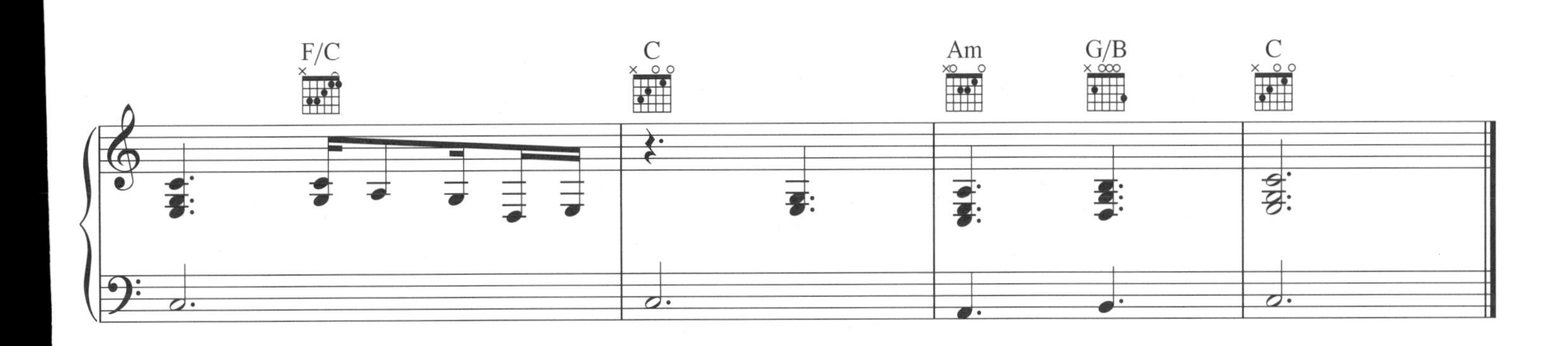
F/C
C
Am
G/B
C

LONG WAY FROM HOME

Words and Music by JEREMY FRAITES
and WESLEY SCHULTZ

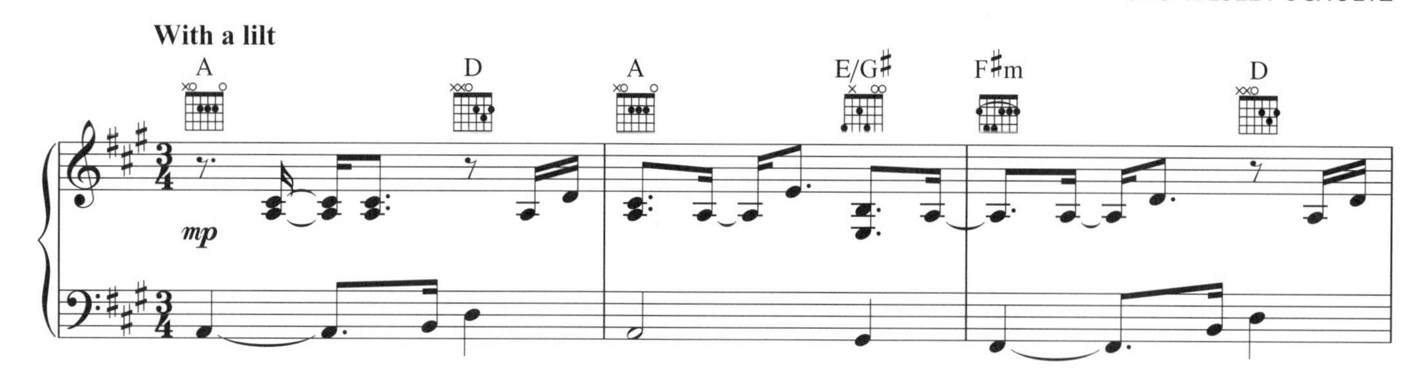

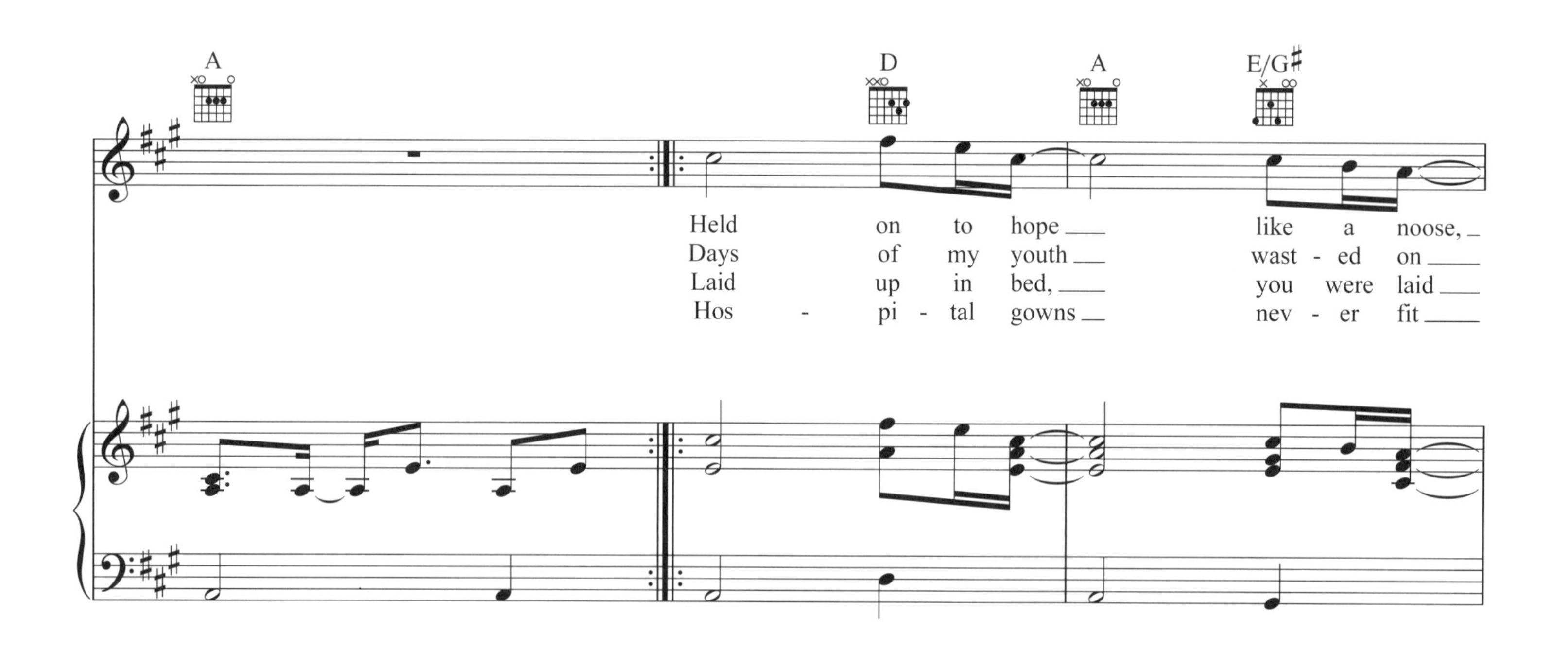

A
E/G♯
F♯m
D
A
take no mer - cy on him.
from the hand you were dealt. I
like you're hold - ing your breath. I
did - n't do an - y good.

F♯m
D
A
F♯m
D
Poi - soned his blood and burnt out his
flew far a - way, as far as I could
prayed you could sleep, sleep like a
More mor - phine, the last words you

A
F♯m
D
A
E
throat. E - nough is e - nough, he's a long
go Your time is run - ning out, and I'm a long
stone. You're right next to me but you're a long
moaned. At last I was sure that you weren't far

F♯m
D
A
D
A
E/G♯
way from home.
way from home.
way from home.
a - way from home.
F♯m
D
1
A
2, 3
A
D
A
E/G♯
F♯m
D
A
4
A
D
A
E/G♯
F♯m
D
A

SICK IN THE HEAD

Words and Music by JEREMY FRAITES
and WESLEY SCHULTZ

Gsus
3fr
Gsus2
G
They're writ - ing my his - to - ry:
G6
Gmaj7(no3)
think some - bod - y should have asked me;
G
ev - 'ry - one was safe in their beds,
their beds.
And I say
Csus2
3fr
Em7
I won't live,
won't live like them.
I don't know
if it's al - right with you,

1
D(add4)/F♯
2fr
but
Ev - 'ry - one, they're all see - ing red.
G
2
D(add4)/F♯
2fr
I'll be gone; a
ghost will be here in my stead,
G
my stead, and I said,
G5
3fr
"I can't live life un - der - neath it all.
I will not be here for - ev - er, dear.

C5
3fr
C/G
G
D/G
Ev - 'ry - one is old - er now and gone."
Let's just make this count a lot in here.
G
Gsus
3fr
Gsus2
G
Em
D(add4)/F♯
2fr
G

Em7
Cmaj7/E
Am/G
G
E5
D
G
G5
3fr

MY EYES

Words and Music by JEREMY FRAITES,
WESLEY SCHULTZ and NEYLA PEKAREK

* Recorded a half-step lower

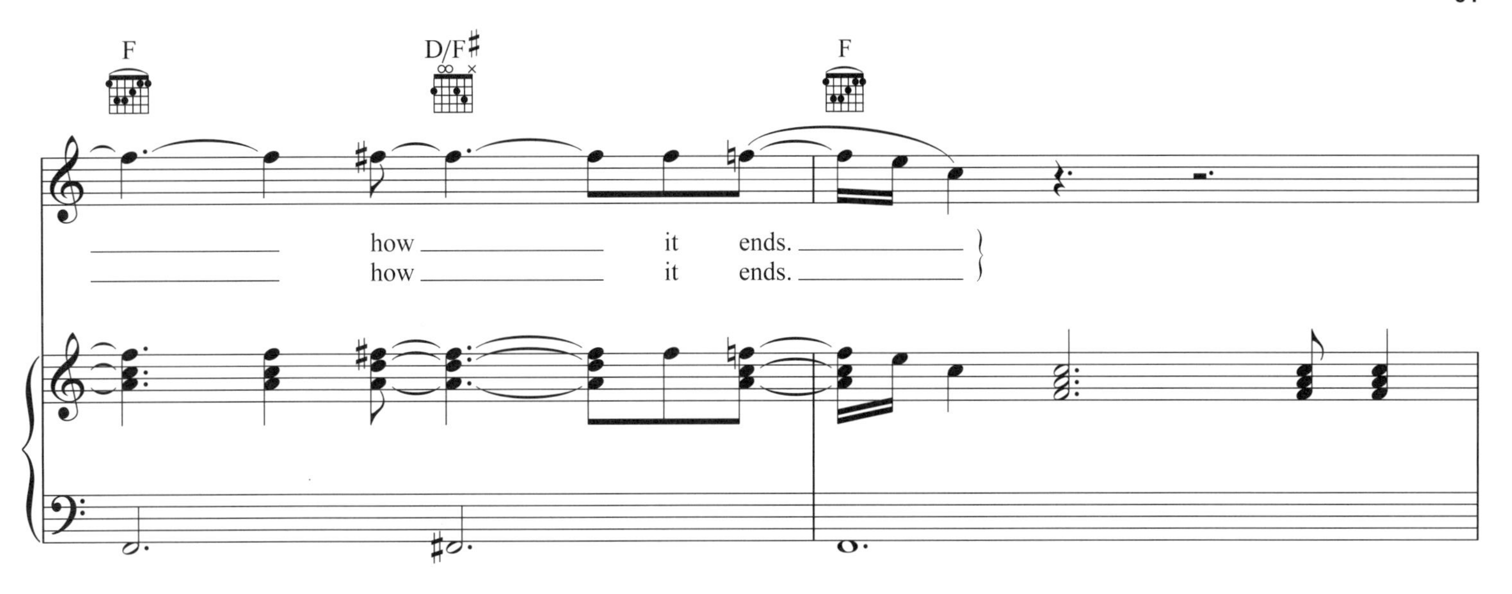
F
D/F♯
F
how it ends.
how it ends.

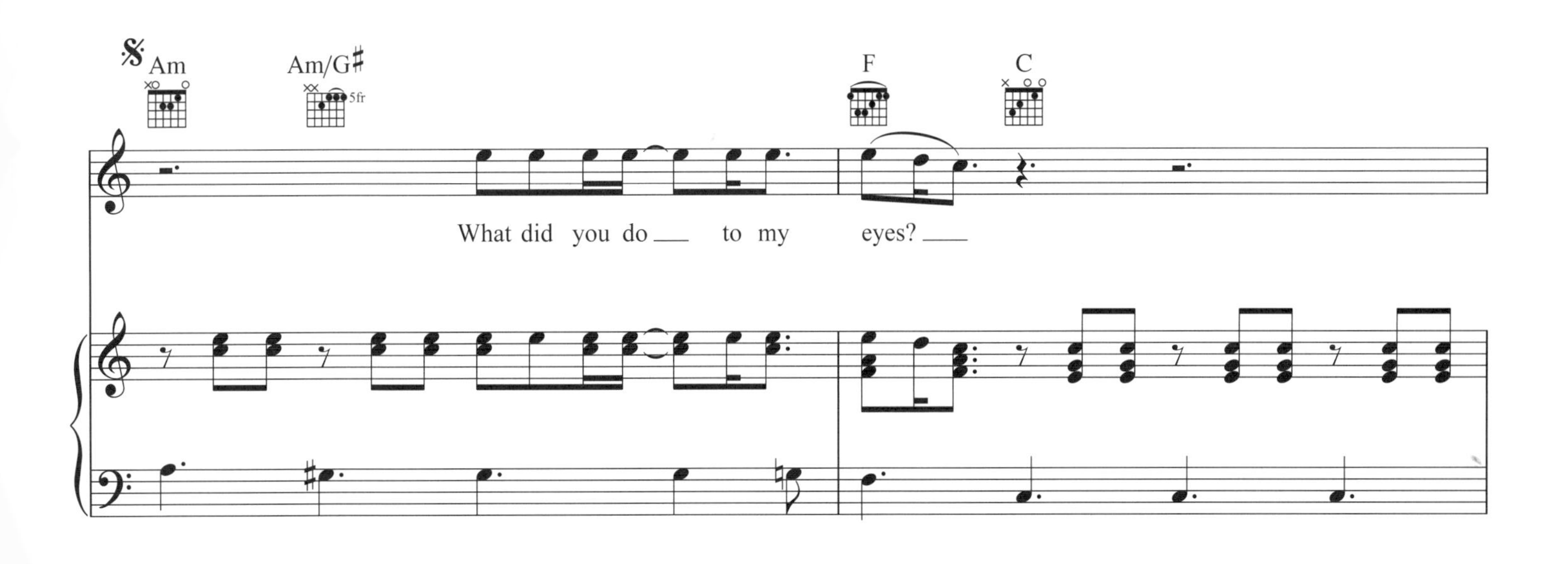
Am
Am/G♯
5fr
F
C
What did you do to my eyes?

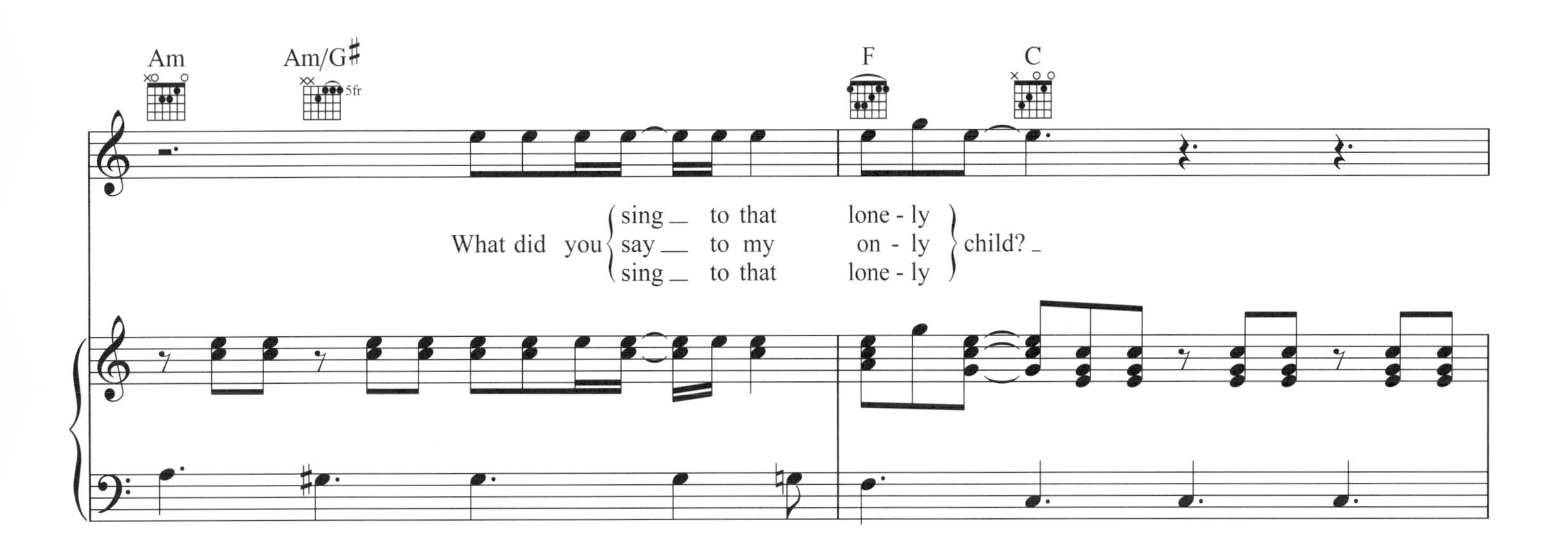
Am
Am/G♯
5fr
F
C
What did you sing to that lone - ly child?
say to my on - ly
sing to that lone - ly

Am
Am/G♯
5fr
F
C
Prom - ised
it all
your love
it all
but you lied.
You bet-ter
To Coda
1
Am/G
Am/F♯
N.C.
slow
down,
ba - by,
soon.
It's all or noth - ing to you.
The

2
Fmaj7
C
soon. It's all or noth - ing to you.
Am
F
C
Am
F
Dsus
F
D.S. al Coda
CODA
Fmaj7
soon.

PATIENCE

Words and Music by JEREMY FRAITES
and WESLEY SCHULTZ

Pedal ad lib. throughout

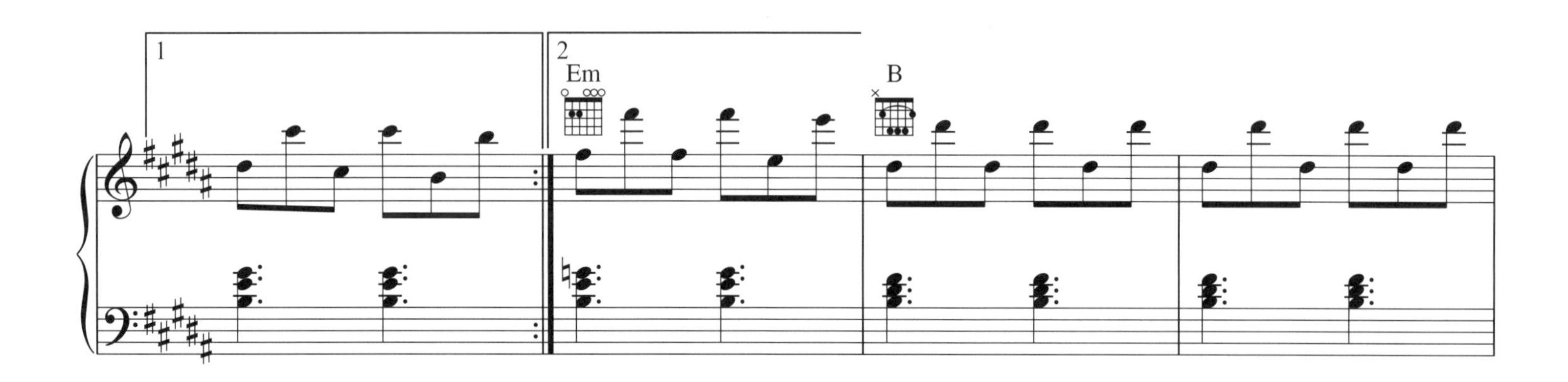

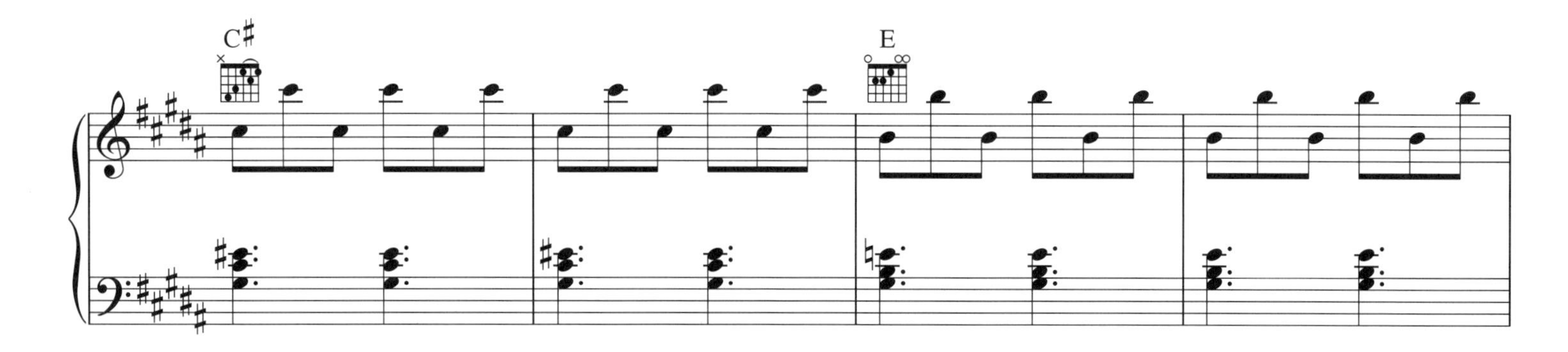

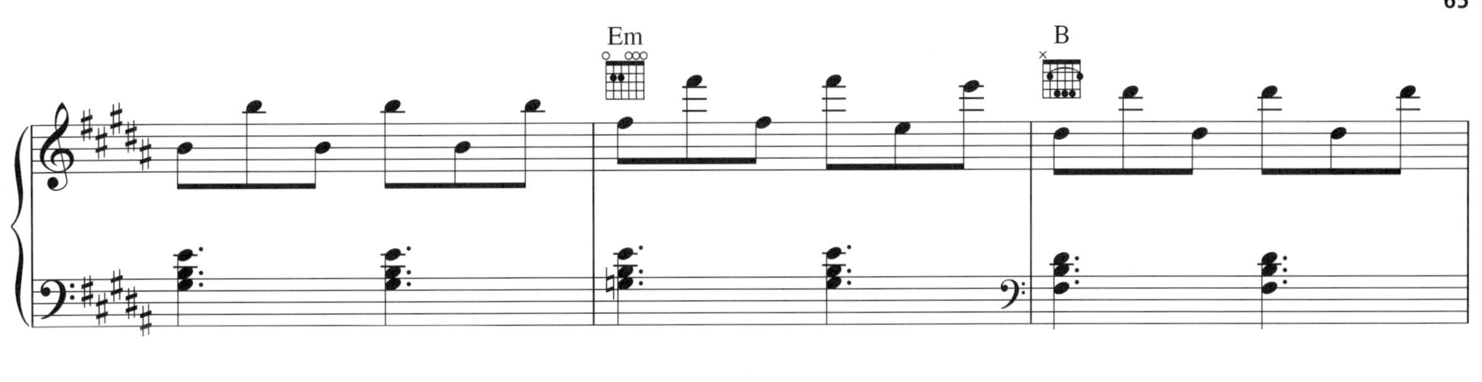
Em
B

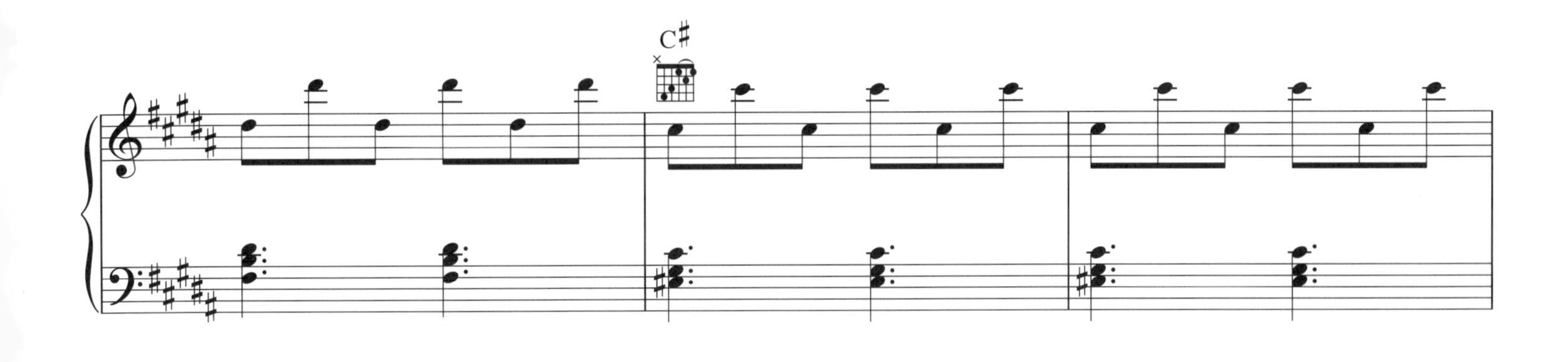
C♯

E

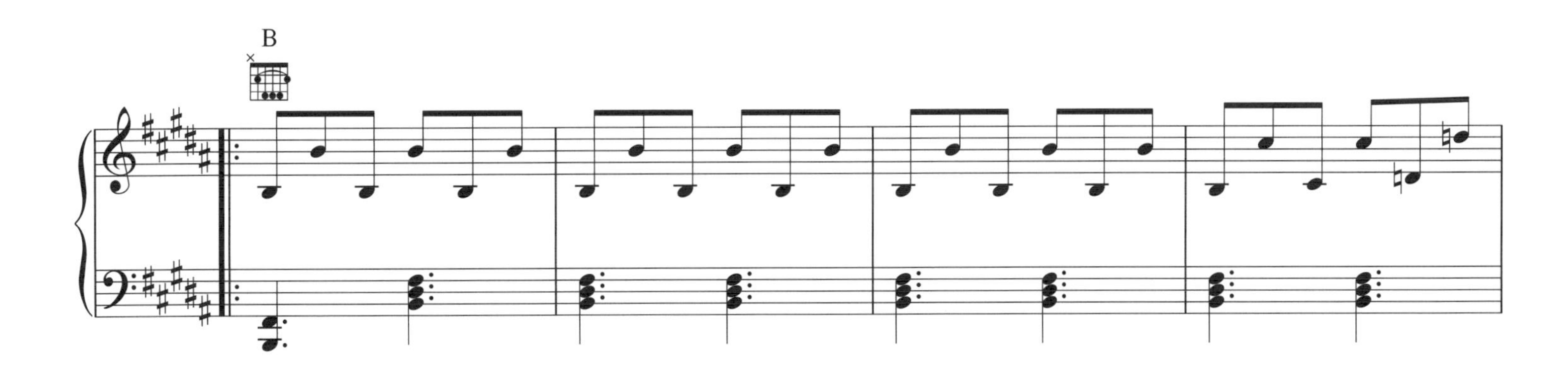
B

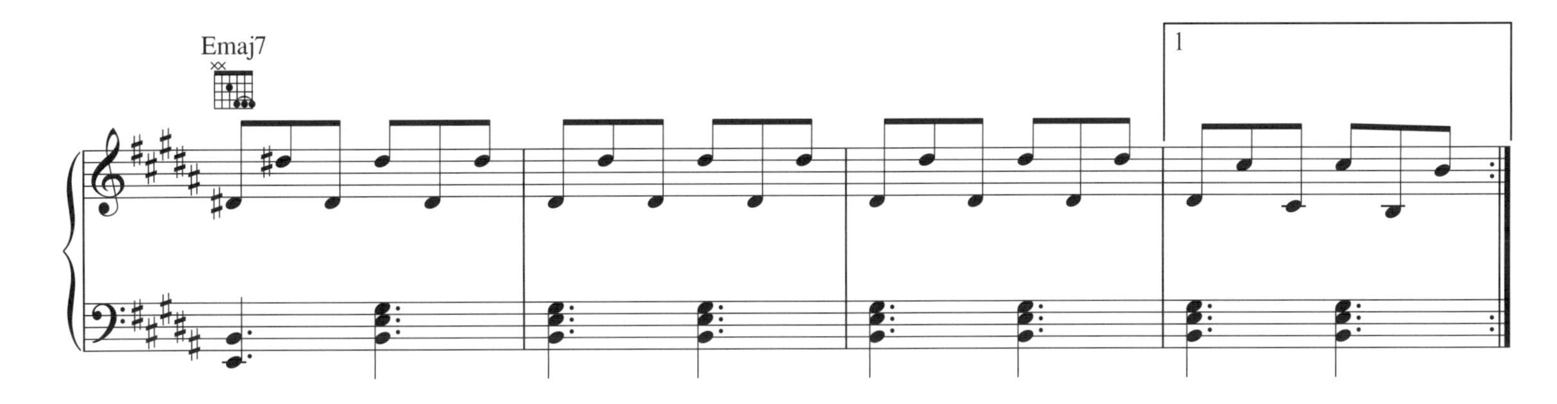
Emaj7
1

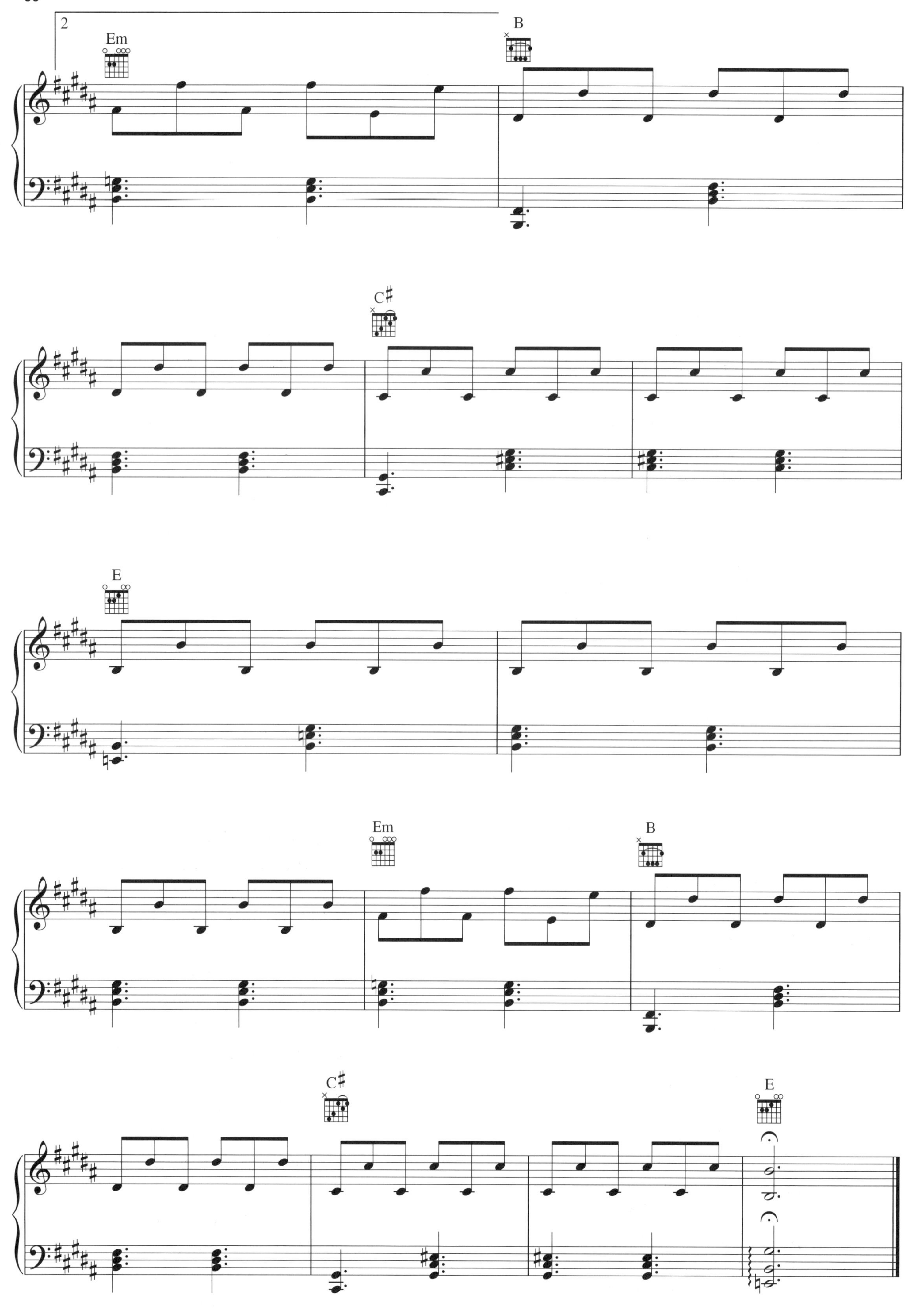
2
Em
B
C#
E
Em
B
C#
E

WHERE THE SKIES ARE BLUE

Words and Music by
ABRAHAM HOVEY

A
I nev - er seen no - bod - y quite like
I would - 've gave all of my best to
It's gon - na feel good like it al - ways
Bm
you.
you.
do.
And if
So if
And when your
C♯m7
4fr
F♯m
you ev - er change your tune, or the
you ev - er need a fool who will
fair - y tale is through, and you're
B
world's got the best of you, you can
give you a love so true, you can
look - ing for some - one new, you can

D
E
To Coda
al - ways find me where the skies are
al - ways find me where the skies are
al - ways fine me where the skies are
1
A
E7
2
A
blue.
blue.
A(add2)
D
A
E
Plant your dreams, lit - tle dar - ling, in a
D
A
F♯m
D
flow - er bed.
Let the sun

A
E
shine in your head,
E7
D.S. al Coda
in your head.
CODA
F♯m
B7
D
blue. You can al - ways find me
E
A
where the skies are blue.

EVERYONE REQUIRES A PLAN

Words and Music by JEREMY FRAITES
and WESLEY SCHULTZ

D/F#
Dmaj7/F#
A
And smoke hangs vel - vet cur - tains and hides her lips.
Asus2
D/F#
Dmaj7/F#
And she hopes to hell it's worth all
A
Asus2
F#m
E/G#
her health risks. I know it was you.
A
F#m
E/G#
A
I know it was you.

F♯m
'Cause ev - 'ry - one re - quires a plan.
E
A
I can give you. It's all been
F♯m
D
E
a sleight of hand.
F♯m
E/G♯
A
I know it was you.

F♯m
E/G♯
A
I know it was you.

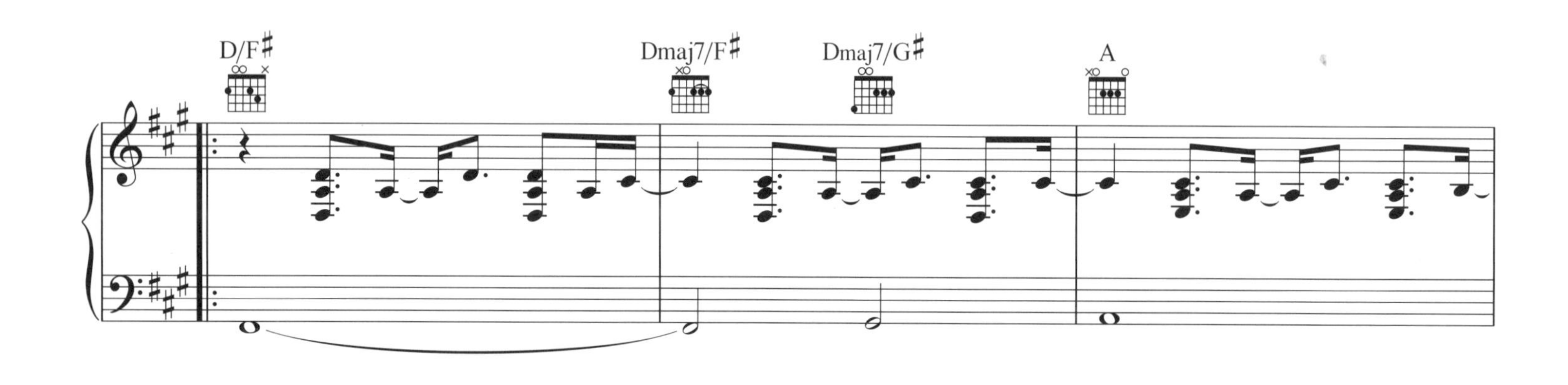
D/F♯
Dmaj7/F♯
Dmaj7/G♯
A

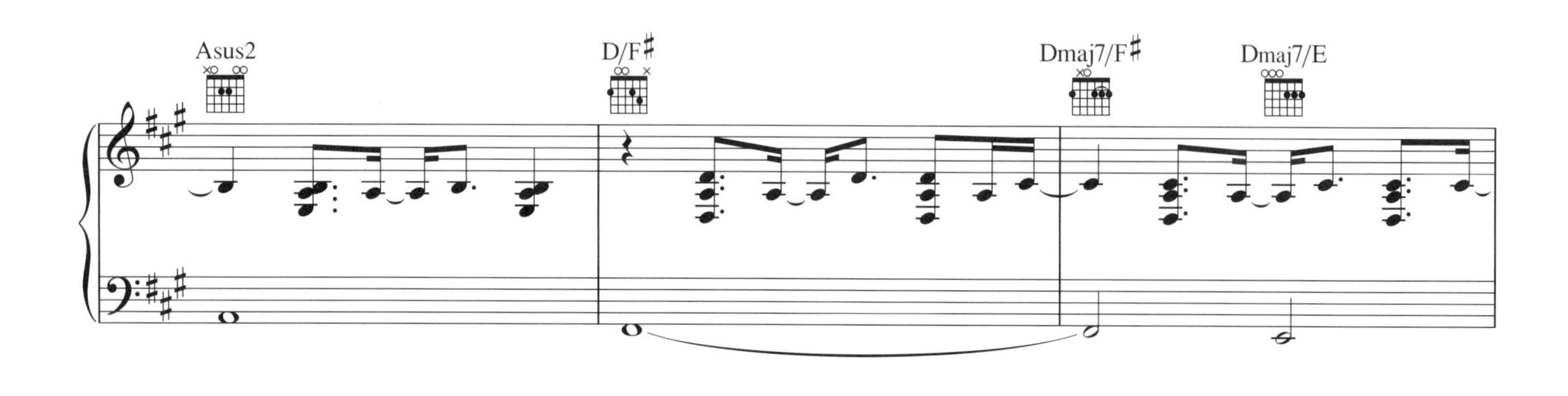
Asus2
D/F♯
Dmaj7/F♯
Dmaj7/E

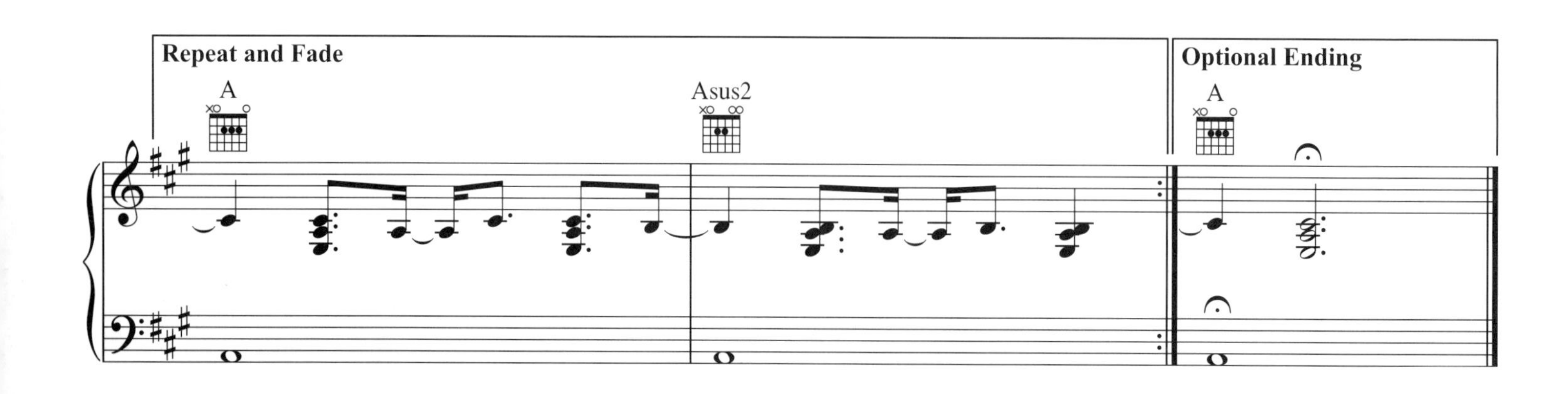
Repeat and Fade
A
Asus2
Optional Ending
A

WHITE LIE

Words and Music by JEREMY FRAITES
and WESLEY SCHULTZ

*Recorded a half step lower.

F♯m
F♯m/E
D
F♯m
F♯m/E
- len, and so have you.
D
F♯m
F♯m/E
D
If we can
F♯m
F♯m/E
D
make it through an - oth - er day
with you be -
F♯m
F♯m/E
Dmaj7
liev - ing in my in - no - cence,
then we can

F♯m
Bm/E
Dmaj7
make it through an - oth - er year, 'cause we both
F♯m
Bm/E
E(add2)
Asus2
B5
need it to for - get this fear. If it's all the same
Dsus2
Asus2
B5
to you, then it's just a lit - tle white lie, then it's all the same
Dsus2
Asus2
B5
to me, and it's just a lit - tle white lie. If I was to blame,

Dsus2
Dmaj9
4fr
would you,
would you still be - lieve?
D
F♯m
F♯m/E
D
F♯m
F♯m/E
D
F♯m
F♯m/E
I don't want you to for - get;
Dmaj9
4fr
F♯m
F♯m/E
just pre - tend that it nev - er hap - pened.

Dmaj7
F♯m
F♯m/E
And it's just a lit - tle white lie.
Dmaj7
F♯m
F♯m/E
And it's just a lit - tle white lie.
D(add2)
D
D(add2)
A
Bsus
If it's all the same
D(add2)
D
A
Bsus
to you, then it's just a lit - tle white lie, and it's all the same

D(add2)
D
A
Bsus
to me, then it's just a lit - tle white lie. If I was to blame,
D
Dmaj7
Dmaj9
D6/9
4fr
would you, would you still be - lieve,
Asus
A
F♯m/B
D
if I was a thief?
F♯m11
E5
Dmaj7
F♯m11
E5
F♯5/E
4fr